WORLD HISTORY Need to Know

SilverTip

The Vietnam War

by Daniel R. Faust

Consultant: Caitlin Krieck, Social Studies Teacher and Instructional Coach, The Lab School of Washington

Minneapolis, Minnesota

Credits

Cover and title page, © Itza/Adobe Stock; 5 © Evening Standard/Getty Images; 7, © Serge DE SAZO/Getty Images; 9, © Bettmann/Getty Images; 11, © Unknown author/Public Domain; 15, © RBM Vintage Images/Alamy; 17, © Hulton Deutsch/Getty Images; 19, © Bettmann/Getty Images; 21, © The Fincher Files/Popperfoto /Getty Images; 23, © CBS Photo Archive/Getty Images; 25, © Jacques Pavlovsky/Getty Images; 27, © Bettmann/Getty Images.

Bearport Publishing Company Product Development Team

President: Jen Jenson; Director of Product Development: Spencer Brinker; Managing Editor: Allison Juda; Associate Editor: Naomi Reich; Associate Editor: Tiana Tran; Senior Designer: Colin O'Dea; Designer: Elena Klinkner; Designer: Kayla Eggert; Product Development Assistant: Owen Hamlin

A NOTE FROM THE PUBLISHER: Some of the historic photos in this book have been colorized to help readers have a more meaningful and rich experience. The color results are not intended to depict actual historical detail.

STATEMENT ON USAGE OF GENERATIVE ARTIFICIAL INTELLIGENCE
Bearport Publishing remains committed to publishing high-quality nonfiction books. Therefore, we restrict the use of generative AI to ensure accuracy of all text and visual components pertaining to a book's subject. See BearportPublishing.com for details.

Library of Congress Cataloging-in-Publication Data

Names: Faust, Daniel R., author.
Title: The Vietnam War / by Daniel R. Faust.
Description: Minneapolis, Minnesota : Bearport Publishing Company, [2024] |
   Series: World history: need to know | Includes bibliographical
   references and index.
Identifiers: LCCN 2023030968 (print) | LCCN 2023030969 (ebook) | ISBN
   9798889165521 (library binding) | ISBN 9798889165590 (paperback) | ISBN
   9798889165651 (ebook)
Subjects: LCSH: Vietnam War, 1961-1975 © –Juvenile literature.
Classification: LCC DS557.7 .F37 2024 (print) | LCC DS557.7 (ebook) | DDC
   959.704/3 © –dc23/eng/20230630
LC record available at https://lccn.loc.gov/2023030968
LC ebook record available at https://lccn.loc.gov/2023030969

Copyright © 2024 Bearport Publishing Company. All rights reserved. No part of this publication may be reproduced in whole or in part, stored in any retrieval system, or transmitted in any form or by any means, electronic, mechanical, photocopying, recording, or otherwise, without written permission from the publisher.

For more information, write to Bearport Publishing, 5357 Penn Avenue South, Minneapolis, MN 55419.

Contents

On the March. 4

Fighting after War 6

Two Vietnams 10

Support for the South 14

Growing Conflict 16

Civilians in the Middle 20

Protests in the States 22

The War Ends 24

North vs. South 28

SilverTips for Success 29

Glossary 30

Read More 31

Learn More Online 31

Index 32

About the Author 32

On the March

Across the United States, young people gathered to **protest**. They called for an end to the Vietnam War. What pushed so many to speak out against a war on the other side of the world? Though the fighting was in Southeast Asia, in many ways it impacted the world.

In the United States, protests against the Vietnam War started at colleges. They spread from there.

Fighting after War

Vietnam was a French **colony** from 1887 until 1954. It was run by leaders chosen by France.

After World War II, the French had to give up control. However, they hoped Vietnam would keep ties with them and French **allies**.

> The United States and the United Kingdom also wanted to be allies with Vietnam. They hoped for political and social connections. These countries wanted to continue to trade with Vietnam.

Not everybody in Vietnam wanted to stay connected to other countries. Political leader Ho Chi Minh pushed for Vietnam to be independent. He wanted it to become a **communist** country like China and the Soviet Union. In a communist country, there is little owned by individuals. The government controls most things.

Ho Chi Minh was a famous leader in Vietnam. He learned about communism when he studied in France and the Soviet Union. Ho Chi Minh returned to Vietnam in 1941.

Ho Chi Minh

Two Vietnams

Fighting broke out over how Vietnam would be run. Some Vietnamese agreed with Ho Chi Minh. They wanted Vietnam to become communist. Others were strongly against it. They wanted a **democracy** to choose another way of life. Eventually, the nation split in July 1954.

> France wanted to stop Ho Chi Minh. However, after losing a major battle in May 1954, France left the country. The pro-democracy Vietnamese lost a strong ally.

The struggle for power in Vietnam grew violent.

Ho Chi Minh took control of Hanoi, a city in the north. It became the capital of the northern, communist half of the country.

Leaders in southern Vietnam were against communism. They were led by a man named Ngo Dinh Diem. Saigon was the capital in the south. The two sides were at war.

Not everyone in the north was pro-communism. There were also some in southern Vietnam that didn't agree with democracy. The Viet Cong was a group in the south that fought for communism.

Support for the South

Other countries soon got involved in Vietnam's war. The United States sent money and **advisers** to southern Vietnam. They were trying to stop the spread of communism around the world. The United States was locked in the Cold War against the Soviet Union over communism at the time.

> The United States and Soviet Union didn't use weapons during the Cold War. However, they were both involved in other wars. Their support of opposite sides made the Vietnam War a proxy war.

Growing Conflict

In early 1965, the United States started sending troops to Vietnam. However, these soldiers didn't make as much of an impact as the United States had hoped they would.

Vietnam is a country with a lot of jungles. The U.S. soldiers were not used to this kind of environment.

> The United States hoped their soldiers would end the war quickly. However, the fight was harder than they had thought it would be.

Other countries sent soldiers to help the south, too. Fighters from South Korea, Australia, and New Zealand joined the war.

The northern Vietnamese also got help. The Soviet Union and China sent money and supplies to help the communist cause.

> Some nearby countries wanted to stay **neutral** in the war. However, fighting soon spilled across borders. The United States bombed neighboring Cambodia and Laos after Northern Vietnamese soldiers moved through those countries.

Australian soldiers in Vietnam

Civilians in the Middle

As more countries entered the war, the fighting took a toll on the people of Vietnam. Bombs from both sides killed **civilians** and destroyed their land.

Many civilians did not want to pick a side. They were afraid of what either side would do if they helped their enemy.

> Before the war, most people in South Vietnam lived in the countryside. That was where most of the fighting took place. As many as four million Vietnamese people left their homes during the war.

Many Vietnamese civilians moved to cities.

Protests in the States

Back in the United States, people saw the suffering of the Vietnamese people on the news. Many became angry that U.S. soldiers were killing people in another country. They thought the fight against communism wasn't worth it. Americans began protesting for an end to the war.

> People grew angry about the death of U.S. soldiers in Vietnam, too. The United States sent almost 3 million soldiers to fight in the country. About 58,000 died.

The Vietnam War was the first war shown regularly on the television news.

The War Ends

Facing growing pressure, the United States government started pulling soldiers from Vietnam in July 1969. Then in January 1973, the North and South agreed to stop fighting. South Vietnam **surrendered** two years later. The war officially ended in 1975 after the North took control of Saigon.

> The northern takeover of Saigon is also known as the Fall of Saigon. It ended the war. Communist Vietnam had won.

Saigon was renamed Ho Chi Minh City.

After much fighting, Vietnam had become a single country. The communist Vietnamese government treated the people of South Vietnam very harshly. Many were forced to leave their homes. Some fled the country. The impacts of the war would be felt for years to come.

> The United States lost some global power after the war. Many people had thought the United States was unbeatable. The country's failure in Vietnam proved that was not the case.

North vs. South

The Vietnam War was in many ways a civil war. It was fought over a disagreement at home. However, many countries took sides.

SilverTips for SUCCESS

★ SilverTips for REVIEW

Review what you've learned. Use the text to help you.

Define key terms

communism
democracy
Ho Chi Minh
North Vietnam
South Vietnam

Check for understanding

What were the main differences between what North Vietnam and South Vietnam wanted?

Who was Ho Chi Minh?

Explain why the United States got involved in the Vietnam War and why the country left.

Think deeper

How might the world be different if the war in Vietnam ended with a South Vietnam victory?

★ SilverTips on TEST-TAKING

- **Make a study plan.** Ask your teacher what the test is going to cover. Then, set aside time to study a little bit every day.

- **Read all the questions carefully.** Be sure you know what is being asked.

- **Skip any questions** you don't know how to answer right away. Mark them and come back later if you have time.

Glossary

advisers people who give opinions and suggestions about things

allies people or groups joined together in order to get or give help

civilians people who are not in the military

colony an area that has been settled by people from another country and is ruled by that country

communist a type of government where individuals do not own goods and property

democracy a form of government where the people choose leaders by voting

neutral not taking sides

protest to show strong disapproval of something at a public event with other people

surrendered gave up fighting a battle or war

Read More

Faust, Daniel R. *The Cold War (World History: Need to Know).* Minneapolis: Bearport Publishing Company, 2024.

O'Connor, Jim. *What Was the Vietnam War? (What Was?).* New York: Penguin Workshop, 2019.

Spanier, Kristine. *Vietnam (All around the World).* Minneapolis: Jump!, Inc., 2020.

Learn More Online

1. Go to **www.factsurfer.com** or scan the QR code below.
2. Enter "**Vietnam War**" into the search box.
3. Click on the cover of this book to see a list of websites.

Index

civilians 20–21

communism 8, 10, 12, 14, 18, 22, 24, 26

democracy 10, 12

France 6–8, 10, 28

Hanoi 12–13, 28

Ho Chi Minh 8–10, 12, 25

North Vietnam 12–13, 18, 24, 28

protests 4, 22

Saigon 12–13, 24–25, 28

South Vietnam 12–14, 18, 20, 24, 26, 28

Soviet Union 8, 14, 18, 28

surrender 24

United States 4, 6, 14, 16, 18, 22, 24, 26, 28

About the Author

Daniel R. Faust is a freelance writer of fiction and nonfiction. He lives in Queens, NY.